For Theo, Toby, Jacob and Lucy

First published in 1984 by Kingfisher Books Limited
Elsley Court, 20-22 Great Titchfield Street, London W1P 7AD
A Grisewood and Dempsey Company

Reprinted 1985

BRITISH LIBRARY CATALOGUING IN PUBLICATION DATA
Brown, Mik
    Jokes and riddles.—(Animal fun)
    1. Wit and humor, Juvenile   2. English wit and humor
    I. Title   II. Series
    828'.91402'0809282   PZ8.7
ISBN 0 86272 129 6

Printed in Italy by Vallardi Industrie Grafiche, Milan

ANIMAL FUN

Jokes
and
Riddles

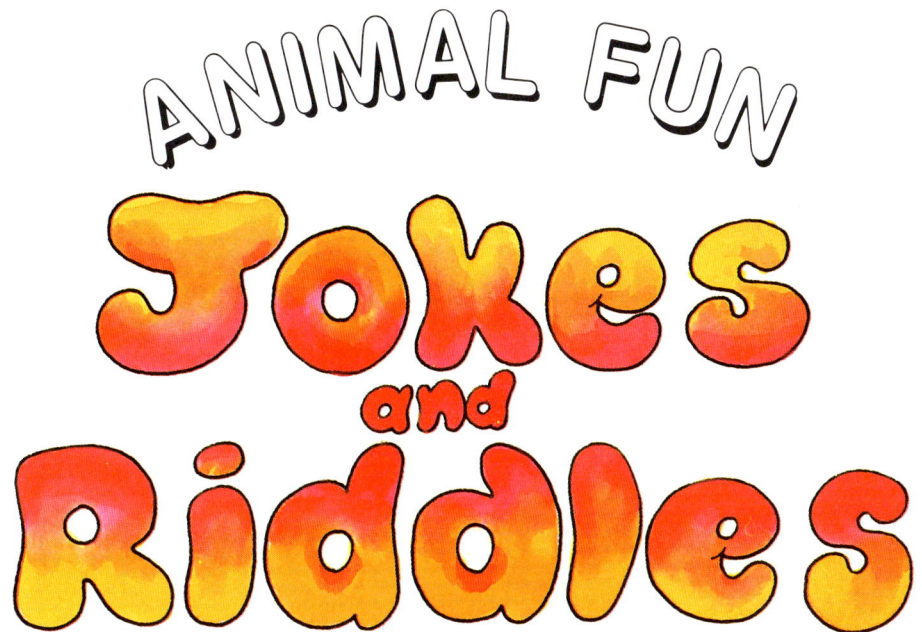

Mik Brown

Kingfisher Books

What's the difference between an elephant and a flea?

An elephant can have fleas but a flea can't have elephants.

Why is an elephant big, grey and wrinkly?
Because if he were small, white and round he'd be an aspirin.

Why does an elephant wear sneakers?
So that he can sneak up on mice.

What time is it when an elephant sits on the fence?

Time to fix the fence.

How do you know when there's an elephant under your bed?

When your nose touches the ceiling.

What do you call an elephant that flies?

A jumbo jet.

Why were the elephants thrown out of the swimming pool?

They couldn't hold their trunks up.

Why are elephants so wrinkled?

Have you ever tried ironing one?

How do you know when there's an elephant in the refrigerator

When you can't shut the door.

What snake is good
at sums?

An adder.

One snake said to another:
'Are we supposed to be poisonous?'

'Why?'

'Because I've just bitten my lip.'

What's green and slimy
and goes *hith*?

A snake with a lisp.

What should you do if you find
a snake in your bed?

Sleep on the wardrobe.

What does a grizzly take on holiday?

All the bear essentials.

SON: 'Can I go out and play?'

MOTHER: 'What! With those dirty trousers?'

SON: 'No, with Tom next door.'

What animal do you look like in the bath?
A little bear.

What do polar bears have for lunch?
Ice burgers.

Where do tadpoles turn into frogs?

In the croakroom.

What's white outside, green inside and hops?

A frog sandwich.

FREDA: 'Will I be able to read with these glasses?'

FRED: 'You certainly will.'

FREDA: 'That's good. I couldn't before.'

What's red and flies and wobbles at the same time?

A jellycopter.

What did the sardine call the submarine?

A can of people.

Why are goldfish red?
The water makes them rusty.

TEACHER: 'You should have been here at 9 o'clock.'

PUPIL: 'Why, what happened?'

What's yellow and highly dangerous?
Shark-infested custard.

Which animal should you never trust?

A cheetah.

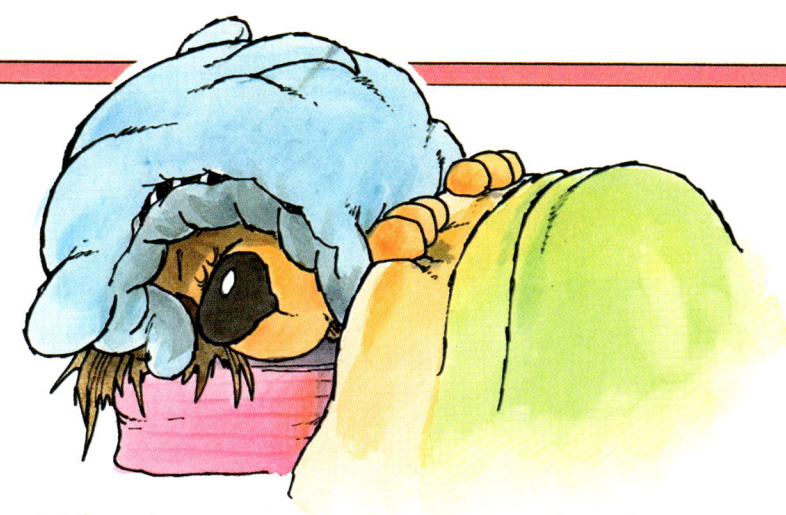

What happened to the lion who slept with his head under the pillow?

The fairies took all his teeth away.

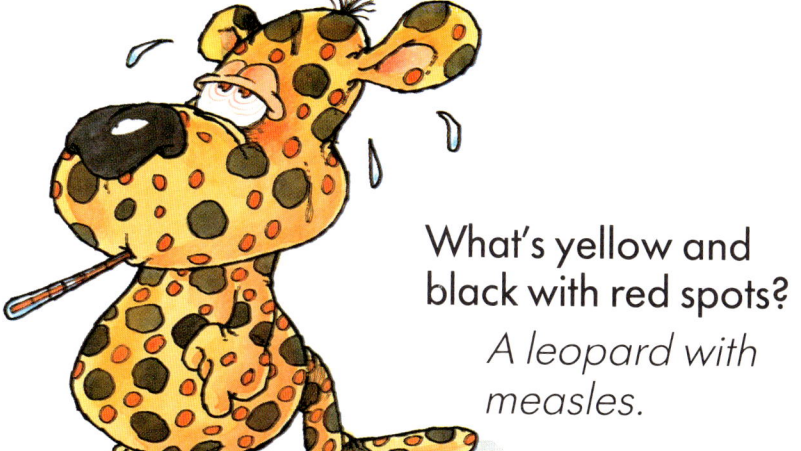

What's yellow and black with red spots?

A leopard with measles.

If athletes get athlete's foot, what do astronauts get?

Missile toe.

Why shouldn't you tell a secret to a pig?

Because he's a squealer.

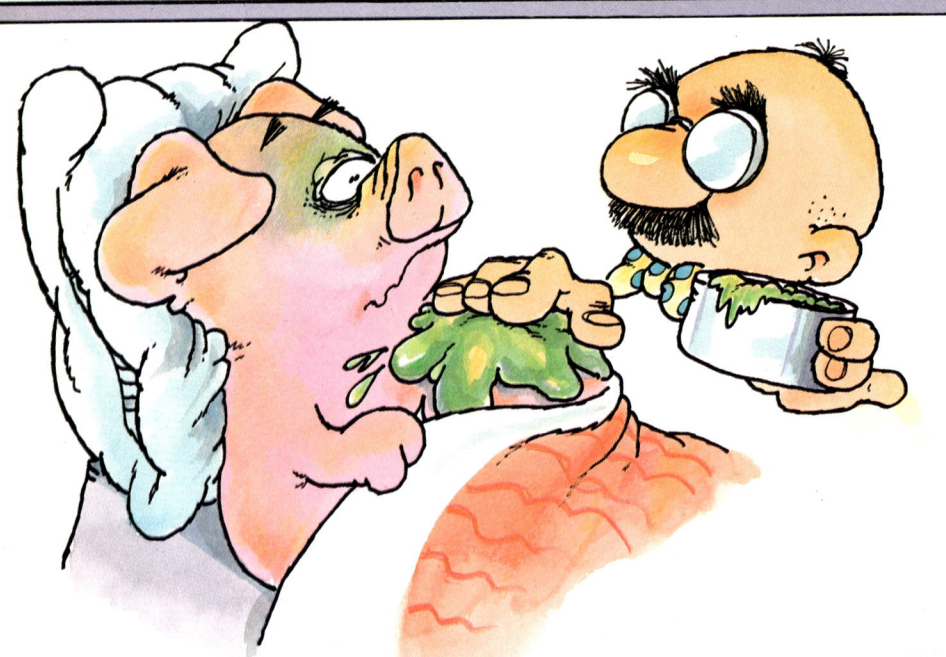

What kind of tie does a pig wear?

A pigsty.

What do you give a sick pig?

Oinkment.

Why is getting up in the morning like a pig's tail?

Because it's twirly.

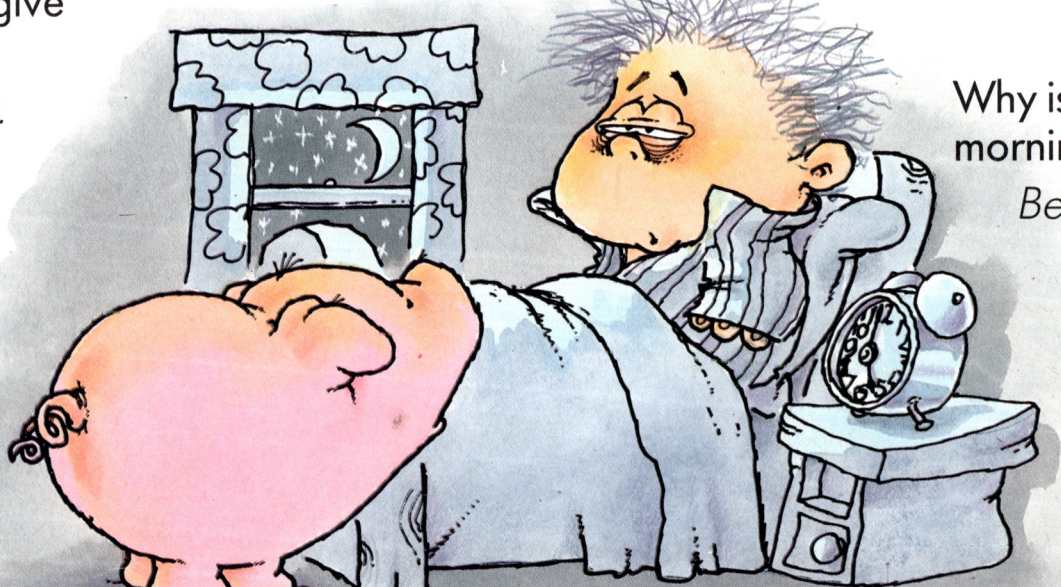

What was the name of the camel without a hump?

Humphrey.

One camel said to another:

'Did you know the cleverest camel in the desert was deaf?'

'Really — who is it?'

'Pardon?'

What animal with two humps can be found at the North Pole?

A lost camel.

'Waiter, this soup tastes funny.'

'Then why aren't you laughing?'

'Waiter, what's this fly doing in my soup?'

'Looks like it's learning to swim, sir.'

'Waiter, there's a small slug on this lettuce!'

'Sorry, sir, shall I get you a bigger one?'

'Waiter, bring me something to eat, and make it snappy.'

'How about a crocodile sandwich, sir?'

'Waiter, your thumb is in my soup.'

That's okay, madam, it's not hot.

'Waiter, there's a fly in my soup!'

'Don't worry, that spider on your bread will soon get rid of it.'

'Waiter, there's a mouse in my hamburger.'

'Don't shout, sir, or everyone will want one.'

'Waiter, there's a caterpillar on my salad.'

'Don't worry, sir, there's no extra charge.'

What did the hungry donkey say when it only had thistles to eat?

'Thistle have to do.'

Who always goes to bed with shoes on?

A horse.

What did the pony say when he coughed?

'Excuse me, I'm just a little horse.'

When did the fly fly?

When the spider spied her.

Why do bees hum?

Because they don't know the words.

How do you start a flea race?

1, 2, flea, go.

What lies down a hundred feet in the air?

A centipede.

What's a crocodile's favourite card game?

Snap.

Have you heard the joke about the watermelon?

It's pitiful.

When the dentist put his fingers in the crocodile's mouth to see how many teeth it had, what did the crocodile do?

It closed its mouth to see how many fingers the dentist had.

What do you call a sick crocodile?

An illigator.

What is a twip?

A twip is what a wabbit takes when he wides a twain

'If I give you three rabbits . . .

. . and then I give you two rabbits . . .

. . how many rabbits will you have?'

'Six'

'Six?'

'Yes, I've got one already.'

How do you tell a rabbit from a gorilla?

A rabbit doesn't look like a gorilla.

What do you get if you pour hot water down a rabbit hole?

Hot-cross-bunnies.

How does a monster count to fifteen?

On its fingers.

What is twenty feet tall, yellow with purple feet and sings like a nightingale?

Nothing.

What's big, red and prickly, has three eyes and eats rocks?

A big, red, prickly, three-eyed rock-eater.

What do you say when you meet a two-headed monster?

'Hello, hello!'

What has a purple-spotted body, ten hairy legs and big eyes on stalks?

'I don't know, but there's one crawling up your leg.'

What's the difference between a huge, smelly, ugly monster and a sweet?

People like sweets.

Why didn't the skeleton go to the party?

It had nobody to go with.

'Doctor, doctor, I feel like a bell.'

'Take these and if they don't work give me a ring.'

'Doctor, doctor, my hair keeps falling out. Can you give me something to keep it in?'

'How about a paper bag?'

'Doctor, doctor, I can't sleep at night.'

'Sleep on the wardrobe and you'll soon drop off.'

'Doctor, doctor, I keep thinking I'm a dustbin.'

Don't talk rubbish.

Doctor, doctor, I keep forgetting things.'

'When did this start happening?'

'When did what start happening?'

DOCTOR: 'Did you drink your orange juice after your bath?'

PATIENT: 'After drinking the bath, I didn't have much room for the orange juice.'

Doctor, doctor, I feel like an apple.

'Come over here, I won't bite you.'

Doctor, doctor, I keep thinking I'm invisible.

'Who said that?'

'Doctor, doctor, I've got a terrible sore throat.'

'Go over to the window and stick your tongue out.'

'Will that help my throat?'

'No, I just don't like the man next door.'

Why does a monkey scratch himself?

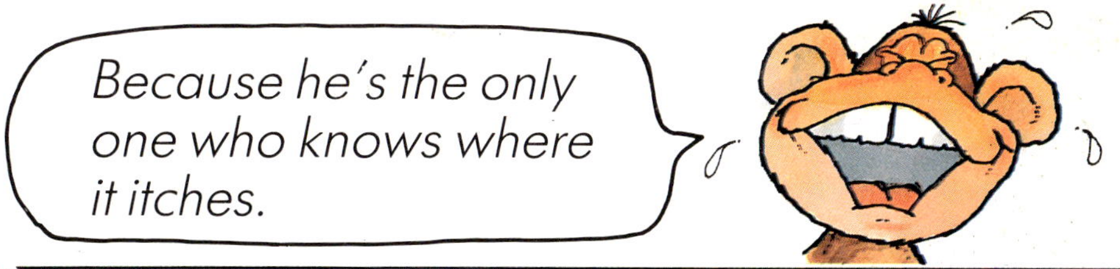

Because he's the only one who knows where it itches.

What do baby apes sleep in?

Apricots.

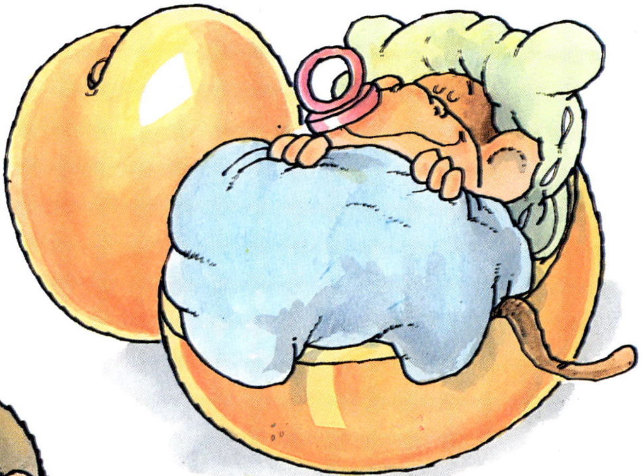

How did the monkey make toast?

He put it under the gorilla.

How do you catch a monkey?

Hang upside down in a tree and make a noise like a banana.

What do hedgehogs eat for breakfast?

Prickled onions.

What did the hedgehog say to the cactus?

'Is that you, Mama?'

Why did the hedgehog wear red boots?

Because his brown ones were at the menders.

If I had eight hedgehogs in one hand and seven hedgehogs in the other, what would I have?

Big hands.

Where would you find a prehistoric cow?

In a moo-seum.

What do you call a bull asleep on the ground?
A bulldozer.

Which cows have the shortest legs?
The smallest ones.

What has the head of a cat, the tail of a cat, but is not a cat?

A kitten.

Why do cats have furry coats?
Because they look silly in plastic macs.

When is it bad luck to be followed by a black cat?
When you're a mouse.

What do angry mice send each other at Christmas?
Cross-mouse cards.

How can you tell
one cat from
another?

Look them up in
a catalogue.

What do mice do in the daytime?

Mousework.

What's white, has four legs
and a trunk?

*A mouse going on
holiday.*

What's brown, has four legs
and a trunk?

*A mouse coming back
from holiday.*

What's grey, has four legs and
weighs one-and-a-half pounds?

A fat mouse.

What did the puppy say when it sat on sandpaper?

'Ruff!'

GIRL: 'I've lost my dog.'

BOY: 'Why don't you put an ad in the paper?'

GIRL: 'Don't be silly! My dog can't read.'

How do you stop your dog barking in the hall?

Put it outside.

'Your dog's been chasing a man on a bicycle.'

'Don't be silly! My dog can't ride a bicycle.'

What does an angry kangaroo do?

It gets hopping mad.

SON: 'Can I have another glass of water?'

FATHER: 'Another? This will be your tenth!'

SON: 'I know, but my room's on fire.'

JIM: 'What's the matter?'

TOM: 'My new shoes hurt.'

JIM: 'That's because you've got them on the wrong feet.'

TOM: 'Well, they're the only feet I have.'

Which animal is always laughing?

A happy-potamus.

What does a hippo have if its head is hot, one foot is cold and it sees spots?

A polka-dotted sock over its head.

How do you tell the difference between a hippo and a banana?

If it's a hippo, you can't pick it up.

Why don't ducks tell jokes
when they're flying?

Because they would
quack up.

Why do birds fly south in the winter?

Because it's too far to walk.

How does a sparrow with engine
trouble manage to land safely?

With its sparrowchute.

What's black and white and red all over?

A sunburnt
penguin.

What's black and shiny,
lives in trees and is very
dangerous?

A crow with a machine gun.

A giraffe, an elephant, a camel, a bear,
a pig and a frog, two mice and a snake
all sheltered under one umbrella;
how many got wet?

None, it wasn't raining.